Quiz Books by Rich Jepson

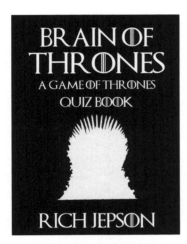

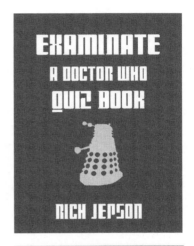

BRAIN OF THRONES

A GAME OF THRONES
QUIZ BOOK

RICH JEPSON

Brain Of Thrones – A Game Of Thrones Quiz Book

Disclaimer: All questions within this book were sourced from reliable, reputable sources. If you find any questions, which you, the reader, believe are incorrect, then please contact the publisher directly so amendments can be made.

Acknowledgements

Unauthorized and unofficial, this book is not endorsed by anyone associated with the Game of Thrones books or HBO TV production. It is purely a fun, friendly trivia book designed to test the knowledge of fans of the drama series.

Introduction

From Castle Black to Storm's End, Slaver's Bay to Dragonstone, *Game of Thrones* is full of weird and wonderful characters, places and stories.

Now approaching it's 7th season, the HBO drama continues to break boundaries and entertain millions of viewers worldwide.

So how much do you actually know about the TV series?

Brain of Thrones is designed to test all levels of 'thronie' from beginner to pro, whether you watch it casually or can quote every line, there is something for you here.

There are 25 quizzes consisting of 15 questions each with a bonus round of 10 tiebreakers. Quizzes become progressively harder as you make your way through the book. That's 385 questions covering everything across the known world of *Game of Thrones*. Test your knowledge and have some fun.

Enjoy!

Contents

QUESTIONS

QUIZ 1 - General Knowledge

1   What is the name of the series of novels, which Game of Thrones is adapted from?

2   Who wrote the novels that Game of Thrones is adapted from?

3   In which year did Game of Thrones first premier?

4   Who plays the role of Eddard 'Ned' Stark in the show?

5   Which character is only capable of saying his name repeatedly?

6   Which character is commonly referred to as Kingslayer?

7   What is the name of the name of the seat of power that the King sits on?

8   What types of animals are used to send messages within the realm?

9   Who fights for Tyrion in his trial by combat in Season 1?

10 Complete the phrase "A Lannister always pays his..."

11 In Season 1, who is the leader of the Dothraki Horde?

12 Varys is said to be the master of what?

13 What network produces Game of Thrones?

14 How many Kingdoms did King Robert Baratheon rule over?

15 How many direwolf pups do the Starks find in the first episode?

Answers - Page 68

QUIZ 2 - General Knowledge

1   Who was supposed to escort Jaime Lannister to King's Landing?

2   What was the name of Sansa Stark's direwolf?

3   How many children is Ned Stark the father of?

4   Who is Joffrey's biological father?

5   What does the brotherhood of the Night's Watch protect?

6   What is the name of Daenerys Targaryen power hungry brother?

7   How many episodes are there in each Season of Game of Thrones?

8   What is the name of the wilding girl that falls in love with Jon Snow?

9   Where in Westeros would you find the Moon Door?

10 Who is Cersei betrothed to marry by her father Tywin?

11 Which one of Jaime Lannister's hands gets cut off?

12 Which character does Kit Harington play?

13 Who is Ramsay Snow's father?

14 What organization does Jon Snow join in the first Season?

15 What name is Petyr Baelish more commonly known by?

Answers - Page 69

QUIZ 3 - General Knowledge

1 Balon Greyjoy is the lord of which Islands?

2 Which character receives a large scar across the face during the Battle of the Blackwater?

3 What is the name of the youngest of the Stark siblings?

4 Who succeeds Robert Baratheon as King?

5 Which character does Lena Headey play?

6 Which character is responsible for the torturing and castrating of Theon Greyjoy?

7 What animal is Brienne thrown into a pit with and forced to fight against using only a wooden sword?

8 Which significant character has their sword hand chopped off in Season 3?

9 Where is the Tully's seat held?

10 Who gave Arya her sword 'needle'?

11 Who marries King Joffrey in Season 3?

12 What was the name of the first ever episode of Game of Thrones?

13 What is the name of the law-enforcement institution charged with acting as policemen for King's Landing?

14 Where does Tyrion's first trial by combat take place?

15 What is the name of the actress that plays Arya Stark?

Answers - Page 70

QUIZ 4 - General Knowledge

1   Who created the white walkers by stabbing a man with dragonglass?

2   Who arrives with his army the day after the Battle of Castle Black in time to fight off the Wildlings?

3   What is Gendry's profession?

4   Who is responsible for melting down Ned Stark's sword to forge two new swords in Season 4?

5   What colour horse does Khal Drogo give Daenerys as a wedding gift?

6   Who succeeds Joffrey as King following his death?

7   What is the name of Theon Greyjoy's sister?

8   Which of the Stark children has a direwolf called Nymeria?

9   Which character does Peter Dinklage play?

10 Which character is renamed 'Reek' after being physically & psychologically tortured?

11 How many daughters does Oberyn Martell have?

12 What is the nickname of Olenna Tyrell?

13 What do the Dothraki mainly eat?

14 Sandor Clegane is commonly known by what nickname?

15 How many men does Theon ask his sister to bring as reinforcements to Winterfell?

Answers - Page 71

QUIZ 5 - General Knowledge

1   What does Ser Loras give to Sansa Stark at the jousting tournament?

2   What is the full name of the character commonly called 'Greatjon'?

3   What 'colour' is associated with King Joffrey's wedding ceremony?

4   Who rules from their fortress at Dragonstone?

5   Who publically executes Ser Rodrik Cassel during the fall of Winterfell?

6   What is the name of Joffrey's sister?

7   What is Oberyn Martell's nickname?

8   Which character, along with his followers, is murdered by The Brotherhood without Banners in "The Broken Man'?

9   Who is known as the 'Red Woman'?

10 Who is the commanding office of the Unsullied?

11 On which of the Iron Islands is the ruling seat of House Greyjoy?

12 What is the name given to characters that have the ability to enter the minds of animals?

13 In order to usurp the three other kings, Melisandre convinces Stannis to burn three of what creature?

14 Who is Gendry's real father?

15 What does Brienne name the sword Jamie gives her?

Answers - Page 72

QUIZ 6 - Anagrams

Can you solve each of the following anagrams to find the name of a Game of Thrones character?

1   ELF IN GLITTER

2   ARK ASTRAY

3   ENJOY THE GORY

4   NORTHEAST NAB A SIN

5   MAYORS SWAN

6   RAN AS TASKS

7   ALERT MY WALLS

8   INSTANTLY IRONER

9   NORTH BEEF TRAIN

10 ANGER RAN YESTERDAY

11 LOOSEN TO ROB

12 EL NOBLE MARTYR

13 RED TANKS

14 BREATHER ONTO BAR

15 OH ROD, OH ROD, OH ROD

Answers - Page 73

QUIZ 7 - The Starks

1 Can you name all six of Eddard Stark's children?

2 What is the motto of House Stark?

3 What is the name of Arya Stark's sword?

4 Bran Stark suffered a crippling injury after he was pushed from a tower by which character?

5 Where is the Seat of House Stark?

6 What role does Robert Baratheon offer Ned Stark?

7 Which of the Stark siblings has a direwolf called Grey Wind?

8 What is the name of Ned Stark's Valyrian steel sword that he uses to perform an execution in the opening episode?

9 Which character is known for carrying Bran on his back?

10 What creature with a distinguishing feature does Brandon Stark have a recurring dream about?

11 How many years did Theon Greyjoy spend living as a ward of the Starks at Winterfell?

12 What crime was Eddard Stark put on trial for?

13 What is the name of the wildling girl who travels with Bran to the Wall?

14 Who does Robb Stark marry?

15 What name does Arya call herself when she disguises herself as an orphan boy in Season 2?

Answers - Page 74

QUIZ 8 - The Known World

1   What are the names of the two continents where the majority of the story takes place?

2   Where is Castle Black located?

3   Which Bay does King's Landing overlook?

4   At the beginning of the TV series, Winterfell is home to which House?

5   Which Islands are home to House Greyjoy?

6   What is the name of the sea that lays North of Braavos?

7   A seat of House Lannister, where would you find the Warden of the West?

8   Where would you find Stannis Baratheon's stronghold?

9   Where does the 'Red Wedding' take place?

10 Who's Keep lies beyond the Wall?

11 Which mountaintop fortress locks its criminals in three-walled 'sky cells'?

12 Daenerys Targaryen visits three cities along the coast of Slaver's Bay, what are their names?

13 What is the name of the vast, barren desert that lays to the east of the Dothraki Sea?

14 Which region is Loras Tyrell from?

15 Which sea separates the two main continents?

Answers - Page 75

QUIZ 9 - Mother of Dragons

1   Whilst pregnant, what does Daenerys Targaryen eat to prove her herself to the Dothraki people?

2   Who is Ser Jorah working for as a spy when he first encounters Daenerys?

3   How many men does Daenerys send to open the front gates of Yunkai?

4   What is the name of the leader of the Second Sons, who kills his superiors in order to align with Daenerys?

5   What is inside a ball given to Daenrys by a young girl in the first episode of Season 3?

6   By what nickname is the city of Yunkai also known?

7   Who serves as Daenerys's handmaiden and advisor in the third Season?

8   What does Daenerys call her horse?

9   Which city are Daenerys and her brother in exile at the beginning of the first Season?

10 Who receives Daenerys at the gates of Qarth?

11 What is the name of Daenerys' army that she purchases from a slave trader in Astapor?

12 What is the name of the house where Pyat Pree holds Daenerys' dragons captive?

13 What kind of merchant tries to assassinate Daenerys in the marketplace?

14 Who performs a curse of Khal Drogo?

15 What is the name of the servant who betrays Daenerys to Xaro Xoan Daxos?

Answers - Page 76

QUIZ 10 - Houses

Can you name each of the following Houses from the description of their flags below?

1 A crowned black stag rampant on a gold field

2 A three headed dragon on a black field

3 A golden lion rampant on a crimson field

4 A red sun pierced by a gold spear on an orange field

5 A grey direwolf on a white field (sometimes with pale green as well)

6 Two stone grey towers and connecting bridge over water on a dark grey field

7 A gold rose on a green field

Can you name each of the following Houses from the description of their 'words' below?

8   Family, Duty, Honor

9   Growing Strong

10 We Do Not Sow

11 Ours Is The Fury

12 As High As Honor

13 Fire And Blood

14 Hear Me Roar

15 Unbowed, Unbent, Unbroken

Answers - Page 77

QUIZ 11 - General Knowledge

1   What is the name of the slum in King's Landing?

2   Hot Pie gives Arya Stark bread baked in the shape of which animal?

3   Who is known as 'The Onion Knight'?

4   Where does Tyrion attempt to send Shae after she is discovered?

5   What does 'Valar Morghulis' translate to in English?

6   Which three characters serve as judges at Tyrion's trial?

7   Who is appointed Warden of the North after the events of the 'Red Wedding'?

8   Who is Gendry's father?

9   What do Pyromancers make?

10 The name Hodor is an abbreviation of what phrase?

11 Who dies as the result of having molten gold symbolically poured over their head?

12 How many swords is the Iron Throne forged from?

13 What creature decorates the fireplace in Balon Greyjoy's hall?

14 Who turns Gendry over to Melisandre?

15 What job did Hodor have in Wintefell?

Answers - Page 78

QUIZ 12 - General Knowledge

1 How kills Balon Greyjoy?

2 How did Tywin Lannister's wife die?

3 What phrase do wildings use to describe red haired characters, such as Ygritte?

4 Who was hand of the King to Robert Baratheon, before Ned Stark?

5 What is the name of the wildling that has the ability to warg into his Eagle?

6 Which character does Lady Crane play in the Braavosi theatre troupe?

7 What is the name of Lysa & Jon Arryn's son?

8 What is the main religion within the Seven Kingdoms?

9 How is Renly Baratheon killed?

10 What was the name of Arya Stark's sword instructor?

11 Who is named captain of the City Watch after Robert Baratheon dies?

12 What type of animal kills Robert Baratheon?

13 What was the name of the woman that Tyrion married when he was young?

14 What is the name of the first character to die in Game of Thrones?

15 Whose head does Joffrey also put on a spike next to Ned Stark?

Answers - Page 79

QUIZ 13 - General Knowledge

1   What is the name of Jon Snow's Valyrian steel sword?

2   Which symbolic items does Daenerys Targaryen catapult against the walls of Meereen?

3   Whilst in Robb Stark's captivity, Jaime Lannsiter finds himself in company with his distant cousin. What is his name?

4   What substance does Tyrion Lannister use to defeat Stannis Baratheon at the Battle of Blackwater?

5   During the 'Red Wedding', Catelyn Stark realizes something is wrong after noticing which character wearing armour beneath his outfit?

6   What is the name of the God Melisandre worships?

7   What kind of poison is used to assassinate King Joffrey?

8   Who is the leader of the 'Brotherhood Without Banners'?

9   Where is Lannisport?

10 Which two characters were getting married prior to the 'Red Wedding' massacre?

11 Who is Jon Snow's mother?

12 When they were children, why did Gregor Clegane burn his brother's face?

13 What are the Faceless Men a guild of?

14 What is the name of the huge weapon that the Night's Watch drop across the face of the Wall to stop the wildlings?

15 Who smuggles Gendry off of Dragonstone in a rowboat?

Answers - Page 80

QUIZ 14 - General Knowledge

1   What is the name of the captain of the guards at The Eyrie who Bronn kills in Tyrion's trial by combat?

2   Who is Catelyn Stark's father?

3   What is the main religion in the North?

4   Which character is known as The Little Lion?

5   Who gives Daenerys three dragon eggs as a wedding gift?

6   What is the name of Stannis Baratheon's flagship that leads the attack during the Battle of the Blackwater?

7   What is the name of Stannis Baratheon's wife?

8   Whilst captured Jamie Lannister tells Locke that Brienne is the sole air of which Isle?

9   What is the name of the pirate-lord that Stannis Baratheon recruits after securing a loan at the Iron Bank of Braavos?

10 What type of tree do new members of the Night's Watch swear their vows before?

11 After being captured Arya Stark becomes Tywin Lannister's cupbearer at which castle?

12 What is the name of Ned Stark's younger brother, who is also First Ranger of the Night's Watch?

13 What is the name of the desert surrounding the city of Qarth?

14 What is the name of the giant who attacks the Night's Watch through the inner gate?

15 Which UK landmark did George R R Martin say was his inspiration for 'The Wall'?

Answers - Page 81

QUIZ 15 - General Knowledge

1 Who does Lord Petyr Baelish push out of the moon door?

2 What is The Hound's biggest fear?

3 What is "Tears of Lys"?

4 What is the name of Stannis Baratheon's only daughter?

5 In which city would you find the Iron Bank?

6 A dozen of which birds where placed inside the ceremonial pie at the purple wedding?

7 What is the name of the castle that Theon Greyjoy is held captive in whilst he is being tortured?

8 What is the name of the only wildling to survive the rear assault on Castle Black?

9 What is the name of the song dedicated to Tywin Lannister in particular and House Lannister in general?

10 What is the name of the prostitute that Joffrey kills by shooting her with multiple crossbow bolts?

11 During the Season 4 finale, where do Brienne & The Hound have a fierce battle?

12 Which character asks Arya Stark for three names for him to assassinate?

13 Who does Tormund develop a crush on in Season 6?

14 What is the name of the battle that takes place between the Night's Watch and the White Walkers in Season 2?

15 Jack Gleeson, who plays Joffrey Baratheon, appeared as a small boy in which 2005 comic book movie?

Answers - Page 82

QUIZ 16 - A Song of Ice & Fire

1   What is the name of the first book in the novel series?

2   What is the name of the second book in the novel series?

3   What is the name of the third book in the novel series?

4   What is the name of the forth book in the novel series?

5   What is the name of the fifth book in the novel series?

6   What is the name of the (as yet) unpublished sixth book in the novel series?

7   What is the name of the (as yet) unpublished seventh book in the novel series?

8   When was the first book published?

9   Which J. R. R. Tolkien story is said to have inspired A Song of Ice and Fire?

10 Which 15th century English civil war is said to be a source of inspiration for A Song of Ice and Fire?

11 What nationality is George R. R. Martin?

12 What does the 'R R' in George R. R. Martin's name stand for?

13 In 1986, George R. R. Martin became a staff writer on which supernatural U.S TV show?

14 In which decade was George R. R. Martin born?

15 On what device does George R. R. Martin write all of his books?

Answers - Page 83

QUIZ 17 - Quotes & Phrases

Which characters that said the following quotes?

1   "A dragon is not a slave"

2   "You know nothing Jon Snow"

3   "When you play the Game of Thrones, you win or you die"

4   "It's the family name that lives on. That's all that lives on. Not your personal glory, not your honour, but family."

5   "The Lannisters send their regards"

6   "I will not become a page in someone else's history book"

7   "Chaos isn't a pit. Chaos is a ladder"

8   "War was easier than daughters"

9   "The night is dark and full of terrors"

10 "Your joy will turn to ashes in your mouth"

11 "Some day I'm going to put a sword through your eye and out the back of your skull"

12 "The things I do for love"

13 "I'm simply asking you to run my kingdom while I eat, drink and whore myself into an early grave"

14 "The man who passes the sentence should swing the sword"

15 "A girl gives a man his own name?"

Answers - Page 84

QUIZ 18 - The Wall

1 Who is known as the King Beyond the Wall?

2 How many watchtowers lay along the Wall?

3 What colour are the eyes of White Walkers?

4 What are the 'free folk' beyond the Wall commonly referred to as?

5 What is the name of the woodland area that lies directly beyond The Wall?

6 Who is credited with building The Wall?

7 What is the name of the town where Samwell hides Gilly and her baby in order to keep them safe?

8 How long is The Wall approximately?

9 Joer Mormont is the _th Lord Commander of the Night's Watch?

10 How old is The Wall approximately?

11 What part of the Wall does Jon recommend be sealed off during the attack on Castle Black?

12 How many of the castles along the Wall are manned?

13 In Season 1, who is the master-at-arms responsible for training new recruits?

14 How tall is The Wall approximately?

15 What is the name of the recruiter for the Night's Watch who meets Jon Snow in Season 1?

Answers - Page 85

QUIZ 19 - The Cast

1 Which actor plays Tyrion Lannister in Game of Thrones?

2 Kit Harington portrays which character in the show?

3 How tall is Brienne of Tarth actress Gwendoline Christie?

4 Sean Bean was born in which English city?

5 What is the name of the actor who plays Robb Stark?

6 Which notable actor in the show starred in films such Alien3, The Last Action Hero & The Imitation Game?

7 The actress who plays Talisa Stark is the real life Granddaughter of which legendary entertainer?

8 Prior to playing the role of Bronn, Jerome Flynn was part of a 90s pop duo with which other singer?

9 Which Game of Thrones actor played the leading role in the 2011 remake of Conan The Barbarian?

10 Which actress in the show played the role of Queen Gorgo in 300?

11 Which Dutch actress plays Melisandre?

12 Which British actress plays Olenna Tyrell?

13 Jojen Reed actor Thomas Brodie-Sangster appeared in which 2003 Richard Curtis film?

14 Which Game of Thrones actress played the role of Margot Al-Harazi in 24: Live Another Day?

15 What is the name of the real life sister of the actor who plays Theon Greyjoy?

Answers - Page 86

QUIZ 20 - Death

Who killed each of the following characters?

1 Viserys Targaryen

2 Robb Stark

3 Oberyn Martell

4 Lysa Arryn

5 Tywin Lannister

6 Eddard Stark

7 King Joffrey

8 Lady

9 Lord Commander Mormont

10 Pypar

11 Catelyn Stark

12 Locke

13 Ygritte

14 Ser Rodrick Cassel

15 Khal Drogo

Answers - Page 87

QUIZ 21 - General Knowledge

1 Who was known as 'The Mad King"?

2 What is the nickname of Brynden Tully?

3 What is the name of Oberyn Martell's sister?

4 What is the name of Jon Snow's mother?

5 What is the name of Stannis Baratheons' table that he and his council sit at in the castle of Dragonstone?

6 In the first four Seasons of Game of Thrones how many different actors have played "The Mountain"?

7 What is the name of Davos Seaworth's son?

8 What phrase is commonly used during funerals of Night's Watchmen as a mark of respect?

9 What is the name of the girl whose corpse is fed to the hounds by Ramsay Bolton in 'The Red Woman'?

10 What is the name of the master of the Citadel who attempts to kill Melisandre by poisoning her cup of wine?

11 What phrase does the Ironborn use as both a war cry and also a formal greeting?

12 What is the name of Rickon Stark's direwolf?

13 What weapon does Samwell Tarly use to kill a White Walker?

14 Who travels with Catelyn Stark to King's Landing?

15 Who does Khal Drogo assign as Daenerys's bodyguard?

Answers - Page 88

QUIZ 22 - General Knowledge

1 Which character does Jon Bradley play in the series?

2 What is the name of the butcher's son that Joffrey bullies and Arya tries to save?

3 Who cuts off Jaime Lannister's right hand?

4 What does three blasts on a horn signal for members of the Night's Watch?

5 Who saves Bran and Meera from being attacked by the wights?

6 What is Ser Loras Tyrell's nickname?

7 What was Daenrys Targaryen going to call her baby?

8 Who is Lord Commander of the Iron Fleet?

9 According to Viserys Targaryen which dragon forged the seven kingdoms together by fire?

10 What was Robert Baratheon's weapon of choice?

11 What is the name of the forest that lies to the north of Winterfell?

12 What is Catelyn maiden name?

13 What is the name of the Septa who Cersei captures and orders Ser Gregor to torture?

14 Who says, "If you ever call me sister again I'll have you strangled in your sleep"

15 Which actor, known for his role as Mycroft Holmes in 'Sherlock', plays Tycho Nestoris?

Answers - Page 89

QUIZ 23 - General Knowledge

1   What was the nickname of the character that Oberyn Martell faced off against in Tyrion's trial by combat?

2   What is the name of Theon Greyjoy's horse?

3   Who resurrects Beric Dondarrion after his fight with Sandor Clegane?

4   What name did Robb & Talisa Stark choose for their unborn child?

5   Before marrying Cersei, Robert was in love with Lyanna Stark. Who kidnapped her?

6   What is the name of the sword owned by Prince Joffrey in the first Season?

7   What are Oberyn Martell's daughters collectively known as?

8   Who fails to hit the funeral boat of Lord Hoster Tully three times with flaming arrows?

9   What is the name of the character that is in charge of the Sky Cells at The Eyrie?

10 What is the name of the wildling tribe that shave their heads bald and engage in cannibalism?

11 Where is Ned Stark stabbed during his fight with Jaime Lannister?

12 What are the names of Daenerys Targaryen's three dragons?

13 Who killed Jon Arryn?

14 What is the name of the Valyrian steel blade held by House Tarly?

15 What present does Littlefinger bring Robin Arryn in Season 6?

Answers - Page 90

QUIZ 24 - General Knowledge

1   What is the nickname of Lord Mormont?

2   Who composed the theme tune to Game of Thrones?

3   Who vouches for Daenerys allowing her to gain entry into the city of Qarth?

4   How tall is the Great Pyramid of Meereen?

5   What language do the White Walkers speak?

6   What name does Joffrey give his new sword that he carries during the Battle of the Blackwater?

7   What is the name of the slave-trader who sells Daenerys the Unsullied?

8   What are the names of the two characters that are being transported in a cage to The Wall alongside Jaqan H'ghar?

9   What are the names of the two swords made from the Valyrian Steel original used in Eddard Stark's sword 'Ice'?

10 Who is the leader of the Black Ears hill tribe?

11 Who are Daenrys and her brother staying with at the start of Season 1?

12 What is the name of the slave-trader who asks Daenerys to allow him to bury his father in a temple in Meereen?

13 Who says, "Wise men do not make demands of kings"?

14 What is Hodor's real name?

15 Who killed Talisa Stark?

Answers - Page 91

QUIZ 25 - General Knowledge

1 Which character has their tongue cut out after singing a song about Robert Baratheon & Cersei Lannister?

2 Who does Gendry apprentice for at Winterfell?

3 Who is the Magnar of Thenn?

4 What is the name of a reanimated corpse that has been raised from death by the White Walkers?

5 Where is the seat of House Mormont?

6 How many languages does Missandei claim that she is able to speak?

7 Who kills Jon Umber at the Battle of the Bastards?

8 Which hill tribe is Shagga the leader of?

9 What is the name of the building in which Margaery and Joffrey have their Royal Wedding?

10 What is the name of the male prostitute who poses as Loras Tyrell's squire when he is actually spying for Petyr Baelish?

11 What is the capital of Dorne?

12 What are the three orders of the Night's Watch?

13 Jaime Lannister actor Nikolaj Coster-Waldau was born in which Nordic country?

14 Who says, "Most men would rather deny a hard truth than face it"?

15 Who killed Orell?

Answers - Page 92

TIEBREAKERS

1 In the first episode, how long, in minuets and seconds, does it take for the first death to occur?

2 How many characters are beheaded in the first four seasons?

3 How many episodes are there where no one is killed?

4 How much, in U.S dollars, has Game of Thrones brought to Northern Ireland's economy?

5 How many people did 'The Hound' kill?

6 How many died at the Battle of Castle Black?

7 What percentage of Game of Thrones viewership is female?

8 In 2012, how many baby girls were named Khaeesi in the U.S?

9 How many viewers tuned in to the Game of Thrones premiere episode?

10 How much does the average episode of Game of Thrones cost HBO to make in U.S dollars?

Answers - Page 93

ANSWERS

Quiz 1 - Answers

1. A Song of Ice and Fire

2. George R R Martin

3. 2011

4. Sean Bean

5. Hodor

6. Jamie Lannister

7. The Iron Throne

8. Ravens

9. Bronn

10. Debts

11. Kharl Drogo

12. Whispers

13. HBO

14. 7

15. 6

Quiz 2 - Answers

1. Brienne of Tarth

2. Lady

3. 6

4. Jaime Lannister

5. The Wall

6. Viserys

7. 10

8. Ygritte

9. The Eyrie

10. Ser Loras Tyrell

11. His right hand

12. Jon Snow

13. Roose Bolton

14. The Night's Watch

15. Littlefinger

Quiz 3 - Answers

1. The Iron Islands

2. Tyrion Lannister

3. Rickon Stark

4. Joffrey Baratheon

5. Cersei Lannister

6. Ramsay Snow

7. A bear

8. Jaime Lannister

9. Riverrun

10. Jon Snow

11. Margaery Tyrell

12. Winter Is Coming

13. The City Watch

14. The Eyrie

15. Maisie Williams

Quiz 4 - Answers

1. The Children of the Forest

2. Stannis Baratheon

3. Blacksmith

4. Tywin Lannister

5. White

6. Tommen

7. Yara

8. Arya Stark

9. Tyrion Lannister

10. Theon Greyjoy

11. 8

12. The Queen of Thorns

13. Horse

14. The Hound

15. 500

Quiz 5 - Answers

1. Red Rose

2. Jon Umber

3. Purple

4. Stannis Baratheon

5. Theon Greyjoy

6. Myrcella Baratheon

7. The Red Viper

8. Brother Ray

9. Melisandre

10. Grey Worm

11. Pyke

12. Warg

13. Leeches

14. Robert Baratheon

15. Oathkeeper

Quiz 6 - Answers

1. Littlefinger

2. Arya Stark

3. Theon Greyjoy

4. Stannis Baratheon

5. Ramsay Snow

6. Sansa Stark

7. Samwell Tarly

8. Tyrion Lannister

9. Brienne of Tarth

10. Daenerys Targaryen

11. Roose Bolton

12. Oberyn Martell

13. Ned Stark

14. Robert Baratheon

15. Hodor, Hodor, Hodor

Quiz 7 - Answers

1. Jon Snow, Robb, Sansa, Arya, Bran & Rickon

2. Winter Is Coming

3. Needle

4. Jaime Lannister

5. Winterfell

6. Hand of the King

7. Robb Stark

8. Ice

9. Hodor

10. Three Eyed Raven

11. 9

12. Treason

13. Osha

14. Talisa Maegyr

15. Arry

Quiz 8 - Answers

1. Westeros & Essos

2. The Wall

3. Blackwater Bay

4. House Stark

5. Iron Islands

6. The Shivering Sea

7. Casterly Rock

8. Dragonstone

9. The Twins

10. Craster's Keep

11. Eyrie

12. Meereen, Yunkai & Astapor

13. Red Waste

14. Highgarden

15. The Narrow Sea

Quiz 9 - Answers

1. A raw horse heart

2. Lord Varys

3. 3

4. Daario Naharis

5. A manticore

6. The Yellow City

7. Missandei

8. Silver

9. Pentos

10. The Thirteen

11. The Unsullied

12. House of the Undying

13. A wine merchant

14. Mirri Maz Duur

15. Doreah

Quiz 10 - Answers

1. House Baratheon

2. House Targaryen

3. House Lannister

4. House Martell

5. House Stark

6. House Frey

7. House Tyrell

8. House Tully

9. House Tyrell

10. House Greyjoy

11. House Baratheon

12. House Arryn

13. House Targaryen

14. House Lannister

15. House Martell

Quiz 11 - Answers

1. Flea Bottom

2. A Wolf

3. Davos Seaworth

4. Pentos

5. All Men Must Die

6. Tywin Lannister, Oberyn Martell & Mace Tyrell

7. Roose Bolton

8. Robert Baratheon

9. Wildfire

10. "Hold the door"

11. Viserys Targaryen

12. 1000

13. Giant Squid

14. The Brotherhood without Banners

15. Stableboy

Quiz 12 - Answers

1. Euron

2. Giving birth to Tyrion

3. 'Kissed By Fire'

4. Jon Arryn

5. Orell

6. Cersei Lannister

7. Robin Arryn

8. Faith of the Seven

9. Murdered by a 'shadow'

10. Syrio Forel

11. Janos Slynt

12. A boar

13. Tysha

14. Waymar Royce

15. Septa Mordane

Quiz 13 - Answers

1. Longclaw

2. Broken Chains

3. Alton Lannister

4. Wildfire

5. Roose Bolton

6. Lord of Light

7. The Strangler

8. Beric Dondarrion

9. The Westerlands

10. Edmure Tully & Roslyn Frey

11. Lyanna Stark

12. Because he played with his toy

13. Assassins

14. A scythe

15. Davos Seaworth

Quiz 14 - Answers

1. Ser Vardis Egan

2. Lord Hoster Tully

3. Old Gods of the Forest

4. Tyrion Lannister

5. Illyrio Mopatis

6. The Fury

7. Selyse Baratheon

8. Sapphire Isle

9. Sallandhor Saan

10. Heart Tree

11. Harranhal

12. Benjen Stark

13. Garden of Bones

14. Mag the Mighty

15. Hadrian's Wall

Quiz 15 - Answers

1. Lysa Arryn

2. Fire

3. Poison

4. Shireen

5. Braavos

6. Doves

7. The Dreadfort

8. Tormund Giantsbane

9. The Rains of Castamere

10. Ros

11. The Vale of Arryn

12. Jaqan H'ghar

13. Brienne of Tarth

14. Battle of the Fist of the First Men

15. Batman Begins

Quiz 16 - Answers

1. A Game of Thrones

2. A Clash of Kings

3. A Storm of Swords

4. A Feast for Crows

5. A Dance with Dragons

6. The Winds of Winter

7. A Dream of Spring

8. 1996

9. The Lord of The Rings

10. The War of the Roses

11. American

12. Raymond Richard

13. The Twilight Zone

14. 1940s

15. A DOS computer

Quiz 17 - Answers

1. Daenerys Targaryen

2. Ygritte

3. Cersei Lannister

4. Tywin Lannister

5. Roose Bolton

6. Stannis Baratheon

7. Petyr 'Littlefinger' Baelish

8. Ned Stark

9. Melisandre

10. Tyrion Lannister

11. Arya Stark

12. Jaime Lannister

13. Robert Baratheon

14. Ned Stark

15. Jaqen H'ghar

Quiz 18 - Answers

1. Mance Rayder

2. 19

3. Blue

4. Wildlings

5. The Haunted Forest

6. Bran The Builder

7. Mole's Town

8. 300 miles

9. 997th

10. 8,000 years old

11. The Tunnel

12. 3

13. Ser Alliser Thorne

14. 700ft

15. Yoren

Quiz 19 - Answers

1. Peter Dinklage

2. Jon Snow

3. 1.91m / 6 ft 3 in

4. Sheffield

5. Richard Madden

6. Charles Dance

7. Charlie Chaplin

8. Robson Green

9. Jason Momoa

10. Lena Headey

11. Carice van Houten

12. Diana Rigg

13. Love Actually

14. Michelle Fairley

15. Lily Allen

Quiz 20 - Answers

1 Khal Drogo

2 Roose Bolton

3 Gregor Clegane

4 Petyr Baelish

5 Tyrion Lannister

6 Ser Ilyn Payne

7 Olenna Tyrell & Littlefinger

8 Ned Stark

9 Rast

10 Ygritte

11 Black Walder Rivers

12 Hodor (after Bran warged into him)

13 Olly

14 Theon Greyjoy

15 Daenerys Targaryen

Quiz 21 - Answers

1 Aerys Targaryen

2 The Blackfish

3 Elia Martell

4 Wylla

5 The Painted Table

6 3

7 Matthos Seaworth

8 And Now His Watch Is Ended

9 Myranda

10 Cressen

11 What Is Dead May Never Die

12 Shaggydog

13 A dragonglass dagger

14 Rodrick Cassel

15 Rakharo

Quiz 22 - Answers

1   Samwell Tarley

2   Mycah

3   Locke

4   White Walkers

5   Benjen Stark

6   Knight of Flowers

7   Rhaego

8   Victarion Greyjoy

9   Balerion

10 War Hammer

11 Wolfswood

12 Tully

13 Septa Unella

14 Cersei Lannister

15 Mark Gatiss

Quiz 23 - Answers

1   The Mountain

2   Smiler

3   Thoros of Myr

4   Eddard

5   Rhaegar Targaryen

6   Lion's Tooth

7   Sand Snakes

8   Edmure Tully

9   Mord

10 Thenns

11 In his right leg

12 Drogon, Rhaegal & Viserion

13 Lysa Arryn

14 Heartsbane

15 A falcon

Quiz 24 - Answers

1 The Bear

2 Ramin Djawadi

3 Xaro Xhoan Daxos

4 800ft

5 Skroth

6 Hearteater

7 Kraznys mo Nakloz

8 Biter & Rorge

9 Oathkeeper & Widow's Wail

10 Chella

11 Illyrio Mopatis

12 Hizdah zo Loraq

13 Catelyn Stark

14 Wylis

15 Lothar Frey

Quiz 25 - Answers

1 Marillion

2 Tobho Mott

3 Styr

4 A Wight

5 Bear Island

6 19

7 Tormund

8 The Stone Crows

9 Great Sept of Baelor

10 Olyvar

11 Sunspear

12 Builder, Ranger, Steward

13 Denmark

14 Tyrion Lannister

15 Jon Snow

TIEBREAKER ANSWERS

1   6m 58s

2   4

3   2

4   $100million

5   18

6   86

7   42%

8   146

9   2.2million

10 $6million

18843665R00054

Printed in Great Britain
by Amazon